PARAMAHANSA YOGANANDA
(1893–1952)

How-to-Live Series

PARAMAHANSA
YOGANANDA

TO BE
VICTORIOUS
IN LIFE

Self-Realization Fellowship
FOUNDED 1920
Paramahansa Yogananda

ABOUT THIS BOOK: The lectures in *To Be Victorious in Life* were originally published by Self-Realization Fellowship in its quarterly magazine *Self-Realization,* which was founded by Paramahansa Yogananda in 1925. These talks were given at Self-Realization Fellowship International Headquarters in Los Angeles and at the SRF Temple in Encinitas, California; and were recorded stenographically by Sri Daya Mata, one of Paramahansa Yogananda's earliest and closest disciples.

Authorized by the International Publications Council of
SELF-REALIZATION FELLOWSHIP
3880 San Rafael Avenue
Los Angeles, California 90065-3298

The Self-Realization Fellowship name and emblem (shown above) appear on all SRF books, recordings, and other publications, assuring the reader that a work originates with the society established by Paramahansa Yogananda and faithfully conveys his teachings.

Library of Congress Cataloging-in-Publication Data

Yogananda, Paramahansa, 1893–1952.
  To be victorious in life / Paramahansa Yogananda.
    p. cm. — (How to live series)
  ISBN 0-87612-456-2 (trade paperback : alk. paper)
1. Self-Realization Fellowship. 2. Self-realization—Religious aspects. 3. Spiritual Life. I. Title. II. Series.
  BP605.S4 Y617 2002
  294.5'44—dc21

                    2002008197

Printed in the United States of America
13468-54321

CONTENTS

PREFACE

"Self-realization is the knowing—in body, mind, and soul—that we are one with the omnipresence of God; that we do not have to pray that it come to us, that we are not merely near it at all times, but that God's omnipresence is our omnipresence; that we are just as much a part of Him now as we ever will be. All we have to do is improve our knowing."

— Paramahansa Yogananda

In his "how-to-live" teachings, Paramahansa Yogananda has given to people of all cultures, races, and creeds the means to free themselves from physical, mental, and spiritual inharmonies—to create for themselves a life of enduring happiness and all-round success.

The books in this series present Paramahansaji's how-to-live wisdom on many subjects, providing readers with spiritual insight and practical keys for bringing into daily life the inner balance and harmony that is the essence of yoga. Through the practice of meditation and the universal principles of right action and right attitude highlighted in these books, one can experience every moment as an opportunity to grow in awareness of the Divine.

While each book addresses a distinct topic, one message resonates throughout the series: *Seek God first.* Whether speaking of creating fulfilling relationships, raising spiritual children, overcoming self-defeating habits, or any of the other myriad goals and challenges of modern living, Paramahansa Yogananda again and again refocuses our attention towards life's highest attainment: Self-realization—knowing our true nature as divine beings. Through his inspiration and encouragement, we learn how to live a truly victorious life—transcending limitations, fear, and suffering—by awakening to the infinite power and joy of our real Self: the soul.

— *Self-Realization Fellowship*

To Be Victorious in Life

PART I

Expanding Your Consciousness for All-Round Success

The door to the kingdom of heaven is in the subtle center of transcendent consciousness at the point between the two eyebrows. If you focus your attention on that seat of concentration, you will find tremendous spiritual strength and help from within. Feel that your

Compilation from talks on this subject given in October-November 1939.

consciousness is expanding in divine consciousness. Feel that there are no barriers, no attachments to the body, but that you are moving on and on into the kingdom of God, which can be entered through the spiritual eye.*

Pray with me: "Heavenly Father, open my spiritual eye so that I can enter into Thy kingdom of omnipresence. Father, do not leave me behind in this mortal world of misery; lead me from darkness to light, from death to immortality, from ignorance to endless wisdom, from sorrow to eternal joy."

---

* The single eye of intuition and omnipresent perception at the Christ (*Kutastha*) center (*ajna chakra*) between the eyebrows. The spiritual eye is the entryway into the ultimate states of divine consciousness. By awakening and penetrating the spiritual eye, the devotee experiences successively higher states: superconsciousness, Christ Consciousness, and Cosmic Consciousness. The methods of doing so are part of the *Kriya Yoga* science of meditation, whose techniques are taught to students of Paramahansa Yogananda's *Self-Realization Fellowship Lessons*.

THE LIMITLESS
SPIRITUAL POWER WITHIN US

As you march along the twisting and branching pathways of life, seek foremost to discover the path that leads to God. In the time-tested methods of India's illumined *rishis,* the universal way has been shown how to conquer uncertainty and ignorance by following the trail of light divine they have blazed, straight to the Supreme Goal. The teachings of Self-Realization Fellowship are the voice of India's masters, the voice of truth, the voice of scientific God-realization, through which the new world will find understanding, emancipation, and salvation.

It is only in God-consciousness that we attain ultimate freedom, complete redemption. As such, we must try our utmost until we receive from the hands of heaven the certificate of our Heavenly Father's acknowledgment, with which He gives us victory over all things.

This world is only a testing place of God wherein He is trying us to see whether we will develop the limitless spiritual power within us or limit ourselves to material attractions. He has remained silent, and it is up to us to choose. I think we will not make a mistake if we follow the teachings that India has given, and in which her masters have specialized. Her supreme gift to the world is the knowledge of how to find God, through step-by-step methods. If you follow the Self-Realization teachings I have brought to you from the Masters of India, you can find God in this life. This I declare unto you. Begin now, before the opportunity is lost and you are whisked away from this earth.

Each word that is coming to you through me is coming from God. And what I tell you, I have experienced. If you practice these truths you will see for yourself that what I am saying is real. I am giving you golden nuggets of truth; they will make you rich in Spirit if you use them to their fullest potential. While the world rushes along, knowing not where, waste not your time in shortsighted pursuits. Why chase after a little money or a little health? These are blind alleys. We appear to be so weak: something goes wrong and we collapse. But behind every bone and fiber, behind our every thought and volition, is the infinite spirit of God. Seek Him, and you shall attain complete victory. You will smile at the world with a smile from within, showing that you have found something far greater than material treasures.

TRUE SUCCESS: TO MAKE YOUR LIFE A GLORY AND A HAPPINESS TO YOURSELF AND TO OTHERS

Very few persons understand the expansion of consciousness that constitutes true success. You have come into this world without knowing what marvelous faculties you possess, and most of you live without trying scientifically to develop their potential. As a result, your life on this planet is more or less uncertain. But instead of living an uncontrolled existence, blown about by the winds of seemingly capricious fate, you can live a controlled existence by which you can schedule your life and make it yield what it should yield: an expansion of consciousness that unfolds in all-round development of the divine potentials within you.

Success is when you have so expanded your consciousness that your life is a glory and happiness to yourself and to others. Success is not something achieved at the expense of others. You have seen, when traveling by car, invariably there are some "road hogs"—those who drive too slowly and won't let anyone pass them. On the highway of life, some people are road hogs. They are stubborn in their selfish ways; they neither progress themselves nor give others a chance to go ahead. Miserly persons are one such example, hoarding their wealth instead of using it to create opportunities and well-being for others. Of all the weaknesses of man, selfishness is one of the meanest demons. By the magnanimous spirit of one's soul it should be conquered.

Real success, rather than being a contraction into self-interest, extends itself in serviceful expansion. The flower, though bound to a stem, by its fragrance and beauty expands its sphere of usefulness. Some blossoms waft their perfume a little distance; others lack fragrance, but still reach out with their beauty to bring us happiness. Trees give of their expansion by providing cool shade and luscious fruits, and converting the waste of carbon dioxide into oxygen for us to breathe. The faraway sun, seemingly small in the sky, radiates beyond its sphere to give us light and warmth. The stars share with us the joy of their jewel-like luster. All of God's expressions in nature send out a vibration that in some way serves the world. You are His highest creation; what are you doing to reach out beyond yourself? Your soul is a beacon of infinite power. You can expand that power from within and give light and health and understanding to others.

Some persons I have met, through the years have not changed at all. They remain always the same, like fossils. The difference between a fossil and a plant is that the fossil is the same now as it was millions of years ago, but the plant keeps on growing. You want to be a living seed. As soon as it is put in the ground, it begins pushing up and drawing sunlight and air, and then it throws out branches and eventually it becomes a sturdy tree and covers itself with flowers. That is what man is intended to be: an expanding spiritual plant, not petrified wood.

You have the capacity to throw flowering branches of power and success all around you, that the inspiration of your life may waft its influence over the entire cosmos. Henry Ford was only one little man who started his work in a small garage, but by his creative initiative he made himself felt all over the world. The same with George Eastman, who invented the Kodak. There is a place in heaven for successful people—and they enjoy that heaven. I am speaking of what I know from my own experience. Every great man who has made something of himself in this world by exercise of the God-like powers in the soul has recognition in heaven.

ACTIVATE THE DIVINE LAW FOR PROGRESS AND SUCCESS

This creation is not run by blind forces. It operates according to an intelligent plan. If God created hunger but didn't think of creating food to satisfy that hunger, where would we be? It is unreasonable to suppose that this world is just a chance result of different combinations of atoms, with no guiding intelligence behind those atoms. On the contrary, it is evident that there is law and order in the universe. Your life, and all life, is governed with mathematical precision by God's intelligently framed cosmic laws. So by the divine law of action or karma, cause and effect, everything that you do is recorded in your soul. Thus, according to the measure of your work, whatever you accomplish through will power and creativity will be your passport after death to the heavenly regions earned by dutiful souls. And when you reincarnate in this world, you will be born with those mental powers developed by your previous efforts.

Suppose one is born in this life with a sickly body and a paucity of material goods and advantages, but still tries unto death to do everything to the best of his ability. His refusal to acknowledge failure creates a dynamic magnetism that will attract health, helpful friends, prosperity, and so on in his next incarnation. Or suppose one makes the determination: "I will do something magnanimous to serve humanity," but he dies before he has a chance to see through to completion his noble undertaking. When he comes back again, that determined resolution will carry over into his new life, along with those mental powers necessary to accomplish that goal. All so-called "hereditary" advantages and "lucky" opportunities in life are not the whims of chance but the lawful result of causes set in motion by one's own actions, sometime in the past. That is why you must start to achieve something now to insure your future success.

To activate that law of action you must be active. Exercise your powers, rather than ossifying in inertia. So many people are lazy and lacking in ambition—doing the bare minimum of work to somehow live and eat until they die. Such a slothful existence is hardly worthy of being called life. To be alive is to be on fire with purpose, to move forward with undaunted determination toward a goal. You must be enthusiastically active, make something of yourself, and give something worthwhile to the world. It is because my Master [Swami Sri Yukteswar] strengthened in me the conviction that I could be something that I made the effort to achieve, in spite of all the forces that tried to stop me.

Many individuals think great things, but do not act on them. However, it is the activity that creates the greatness. Unless you actually accomplish, you are not successful. It is not enough just to think success or think ideas; they must be demonstrated. To think you are virtuous does not make you virtuous. So thinking success does not make you successful. You may say, "I am an admirable spiritual person"; but only if you behave spiritually are you spiritual. All action begins with thought, which is action on the plane of consciousness. To be manifested, thoughts must be charged with dynamic will by concentration and perseverance to rouse the indomitable power of the mind. Thus, to think greatness is a first step, but then you must empower the idea with will and set in motion the corresponding laws of action. "Understanding this, wise men who have sought after salvation, since pristine times, have performed dutiful actions. Therefore, do thou also act dutifully, even as did the ancients of bygone ages."*

OVERCOMING OBSTRUCTIONS AROUND YOU AND WITHIN YOU

It is inevitable in this world of relativity—light and darkness, good and evil—that whenever you try to expand, you will meet enemies. This holds true in all endeavor: The minute you try to accomplish anything, there is resistance. As soon as a plant tries to emerge from its seed, first there is resistance from the earth, and then the bugs go

* *God Talks With Arjuna: The Bhagavad Gita* IV:15.

after it, and then it has to struggle against the weeds that compete for its food and water. The plant needs help from the gardener. And the same is true for human beings. If because of adverse circumstances or inner weaknesses you haven't the strength to put forth branches of success on the tree of your life, you need the assistance of a teacher, or guru, who can help you cultivate the power of your mind. The guru teaches you the art of meditation, of cauterizing the weeds of limiting habits and bad karma that are trying to choke your ground. You must resist these enemies; you must go on trying. Without battle you cannot achieve anything. But neither do you willfully hurt anybody with ruthless tactics to get your way. You use the spiritual powers of mind and will to conquer the obstructing forces and circumstances around you and the self-engendered limitations within you. Then you can be what you want to be, and accomplish what you want to accomplish.

Remember, you have the power to be strong. Right behind your consciousness is the omnipotence of God. But instead of utilizing that divine strength, you have built up a solid wall between yourself and His power. Your concentration is always focused outside, dependent on the material body and world, instead of inside on the Divine Indweller.* That is why you think you have limitations.

STRENGTHENING THE SUCCESS-PRODUCING POWER OF THE MIND

Then what is the way of expansion, the way of progress? It is to look within, to release your inner powers. Each one of you can do so. Start today. Mind is the principal thing; it is the instrument of God by which everything is created. It is most flexible; it will create according

---

* "Ye are the temple of the living God; as God hath said, I will dwell in them, and walk in them; and I will be their God, and they shall be my people" (II Corinthians 6:16).

to any pattern of thought. Mind makes health and spirituality, disease and ignorance. What is disease but the thought of disease? What is ignorance but the thought of ignorance? What is failure but the thought of failure? I have studied all walks of life, and I see those who do not succeed are those who do not cultivate the power of the mind.

To try for success in any worthwhile endeavor is to increase the power of your mind. As your mind power develops, so does your magnetism, the attractive force generated within you that draws conditions and persons that promote success. Worthwhile relationships are important to you. You do not want the advantages of success without friends (be they family loved ones or supportive acquaintances) who will appreciate and help you, and with whom you can share your happiness. The high quality of your mind power and magnetism will attract those friends who contribute to the meaningfulness of your life. Do your part to make lasting friendships by being a true friend. Try to improve your own personality. The Lord has made you something unique. Nobody has anything quite like what you have. You have a face and a mind that no one else has. You should be proud of yourself and not indulge in envy and self-pity. Be a straight shooter, be fearless, be honest, be kind, compassionate, understanding, interested in others without being intrusively curious. The silent vibrations of your mind power and magnetism will speak to others of your sterling qualities.

BREAK OUT OF THE CUBICLE OF YOUR LIMITATIONS

The tendency is to think, "I am what I am. I cannot be different." Believe that, and you are doomed to stay that way! If you reason, "I have this much ability, and I can do no more," you are certain to remain just where you are. You forget that in your youth you were filled with ambition, afire with conviction that you could "conquer the world." But gradually the world closed in on you; you were captured by enemies of pessimism, inertia, and naysaying preconceptions that pigeonholed you and your capacities to achieve. Do not remain in that cubicle for the rest of your life.

There is a way to break free. For a small nation, surrounded by enemies, it is difficult to achieve independence or expand its territory; but that is because the barriers are outside. In achieving mental and spiritual independence, it is not a question of external obstructions. The confining barrier is yourself and the bad habits that you have created. You concentrate on your limitations and the mental hedges you have cultivated. By your own decree you have imprisoned yourself and precluded your development. But whatever boundaries you have created you can undo and destroy, provided you go about it in the right way.

The ordinary man's consciousness is like a small house; that is his kingdom. Perhaps he looks a little beyond, but he has no wish to expand. And some people mentally and spiritually are locked up in a tiny room, their aspirations closeted by a dogmatic conviction of ordinariness. These "walking dead" lack belief in any possibility of conquering new ground.

Do you realize that each one of you is potentially a spiritual giant, a spiritual counterpart to the powerful Genghis Khan, who was one of the most successful conquerors in history. Of course, earthly conquest is not so laudable if it brings in its wake bloodshed and suffering. One may conquer worldly dominions and reign over an opulent kingdom, but still be a slave to misery and fears. To be a conqueror of self is to be truly victorious — to conquer your circumscribed consciousness and expand your spiritual powers without limit. You can go as far as you want to go, past all limitations, and live a supremely victorious existence.

Break out of the mental cell of ignorance that has you confined. Think differently. Refuse to be limited by thoughts of weakness or age. Who told you that you are old? You are not old. You, the soul, are eternally young. Impress that thought on your consciousness: "I am the soul, a reflection of ever-youthful Spirit. I am vibrant with youth, with ambition, with power to succeed." Your thoughts can limit you or they can free you. You are your worst enemy, and you are your best friend. You have all the power to accomplish what you want, if you motivate yourself, if you remove the mental kinks that are blocking the flow of conviction.

THE ANTIDOTE FOR
"CAN'T CONSCIOUSNESS"

I have seen persons who, despite ill health, have made up their minds to achieve something. Their ailing body was always trying to divert their attention, but they overcame that physical barrier and undeterred went on and on, realizing their goal by sheer strength of mind. And I have seen others with wonderful health, but peanut brains. No matter how you try to convince them, they say, "I can't do it." They are stopped by the mental barrier of feeling inadequate. And some people have both health and intelligence, but they do not succeed because they have spiritual barriers of bad habits. Whether from physical, mental, or spiritual causes, failure starts with the avowal, "I can't do it." Such is the force of the mind and the vibratory power of words. When you say to yourself, "I can't do it," no one else in the whole world can change that decree. You must destroy that paralyzing enemy: "I can't."

There is an antidote for "can't consciousness": the affirmation "I can!" Create that antidote with your mind and administer it with your will.

The companionate impediment must also be vanquished: "I can do it, but I *won't* do it." Many people have this mindset, because it is much easier to sit and do nothing. The worst sin against your progress and success is to be mentally lazy. Physical laziness is sometimes forgivable because you have worked hard and the body wants to rest. But mental laziness is absolutely inexcusable; it petrifies your mind. If you forsake "won't" laziness, if you make up your mind that "I have got to do it, and I must do it, and I will do it," success will surely materialize.

Throw out all negative thoughts. Overcome the idea that you cannot do a thing by simply starting to do it. And then continuously keep on doing it. Circumstances will try to slap you down, to make you become discouraged and again say, "I can't do it." If there is a devil, that devil is "I can't do it." That is the satan that has disconnected your dynamo of eternal power; it is the main reason you do not succeed in life. Throw that demon out of your consciousness by your indomitable conviction: "I *can* do it." Mean it, and affirm it as often as you can. Mentally believe it, and energize that belief by acting on it with will power. Work! And while you work, never give up the thought, "I can do it." Even if there are a thousand obstacles, do not relent. If you have that determination, then what you go after must inevitably come to pass; and when it does, you will say, "Well, it was so easy!"

So why should you surrender to inertia and live in a crust of ignorance? Isn't it better to burst that shell of "can't" into the free air of "I can"? Then you will know that mind is all-powerful; anything your mind can think can be materialized. There is no obstruction but your "can't" consciousness. See how wonderful is the way of expansion I am showing you. The words, "I can, I must, and I will"—that is the way to change yourself and achieve absolute victory.

GOD HAS GIVEN YOU MENTAL DYNAMITE

You will never win unless you make the effort. God has given you mental dynamite sufficient to destroy all your difficulties. Remember that. It is the most effective force you can use to be victorious in life, to break free of limiting weaknesses and habits into an all-accomplishing expansion of your consciousness. Are you going to remain a walking dead person, ready to be buried in the grave beneath the debris of your errors? No! Do something in this world—do something wonderful! Whatever you do will be recognized by God. And even if the world fails to recognize you, if you have done everything you can, that infused mental power will remain with your soul. Wherever you go—in this life or beyond—you will have with you that invincible spirit. As the Lord Krishna exhorted the warrior-prince Arjuna: "O Scorcher of Foes, forsake this small weak-heartedness. Arise!"*

I have used that power of mind throughout my life, and I have seen it work. You, also, when confronted by ill health and failure, should meditate deeply and mentally affirm: "Almighty Father, I am Thy child. I shall use my inherited divine powers of mind and will to shatter the causes of failure." Rally those mental forces at night, when the distractions of the world recede and your mind is highly focused and recharged in meditation, prayer, and God-communion.

* *God Talks With Arjuna: The Bhagavad Gita* II:3.

What more shall I say to you? These thoughts are practical; they work. And if you make up your mind to use them, and get busy, they *will* work. You can demolish your difficulties; you can break down the ramparts of ignorance that have enclosed you for incarnations. You will know that as an immortal child of God, death cannot kill you, nor can birth in this fleshly cage completely inhibit the transcendent power within you.* By the soul you must redeem the soul, that no matter where you are, you have at your command the irresistible divine powers of mind and will to vanquish every obstacle in your path!

---

* "No weapon can pierce the soul; no fire can burn it; no water can moisten it; nor can any wind wither it. The soul is uncleavable; it cannot be burnt or wetted or dried. The soul is immutable, all-permeating, ever calm, and immovable—eternally the same" (*God Talks With Arjuna: The Bhagavad Gita* II: 23–24).

MATERIAL ACHIEVEMENTS DO NOT CONSTITUTE REAL SUCCESS

Ask yourself what is the purpose of your life. You have been made in the image of God; that is your real Self. Realizing the image of God within you is the ultimate success—infinite joy, fulfillment of every desire, victory over all difficulties of the body and incursions of the world.

Human life is a constant confrontation with problems. Everyone has a different problem to face: fifteen hundred million people, and fifteen hundred million different problems to be coped with every day. Some have heart trouble, some have colds; some have too much money, some have none; some have anger, some have a bland indifference; but who has happiness? The real measure of success is happiness: Whatever your position in life, are you happy?

The common idea of success means having

wealth and friends and beautiful possessions—the so-called "good life." But material
achievements do not necessarily constitute
real success, because things and conditions are
subject to change. Today you may have;
tomorrow you may not have. So do not think
that just by becoming a millionaire you can
consider yourself successful.

You may work hard to reap success in business, but before you realize it your life
becomes unbalanced, leaving you no freedom
to enjoy the things you want to do, and giving
you such worry and nervousness that your
health breaks down. Suddenly all your success means nothing and you feel that you have
wasted your life. Or by concerted effort you
may develop a healthy body, and yet find
yourself so poor that you are miserable in
being unable to satisfy its needs. You may
even have both health and money, but still feel
that inner fulfillment has eluded you; catering

only to the body and ego will never satisfy the soul. You may have everything, and yet find that ultimately it amounts to nothing at all, because you have no happiness. Unless there is happiness in the heart, you have no success.

However, very few can be happy without possessing at least an adequate quantum of money and health. Most persons must have something to be happy about; their happiness is conditional on outer circumstances, because the mind has not been trained to be unconditionally happy from within. You think you would be happy if only you could acquire all the things you feel you need in order to be happy. But desire begets desires; and satisfaction will never come if you go on multiplying your wants. Before you buy something, you think you cannot do without it; but once you have it, you think little of it as you begin to wish for something better. No matter how often you experience this, when you are in the grip of an impulse to buy something new, again you feel you must have it and will not be happy until you do. Success lies in learning the art of inner contentment: Acquire what you need, and then be satisfied with what you have.

Don't Be Enslaved by Temptation to Live Beyond Your Means

Some people are habitual impulse buyers of things they don't need. They fritter away their funds. Get in the habit of shopping carefully and buying wisely. If you have some extra money, save it; don't "hark to the shark" who is always tempting you to hand over your earnings for some new "must-have" gadget or "guaranteed" investment. Whenever someone lures you with silver-tongued propositions, remember the story about the fox and the crow. The crow had a sweetmeat in its mouth and the fox wanted that tidbit. The fox, being foxy, said: "Please sing for me, Mr. Crow; you have such a beautiful voice." The crow was flattered and started to sing; but as soon as it opened its mouth, it dropped the sweetmeat. The crafty fox picked it up and ran away. Beware of anyone who psychologizes you; he wants something from you. Never be cajoled by anybody's attempt to manipulate you to desire something unnecessary to your real happiness and success.

Simplify your life, so that you are not dependent upon too many possessions. To feed your every desire automatically creates unhappiness. I compare the American civilization with the Indian civilization: All the progressive advantages I wanted for India, to alleviate her poverty and physical suffering, I see here. But I find that most of the so-called successful persons here are just as miserable with their wealth as are the less fortunate in India without it.

Western life is so full of complexities; you

have no time to enjoy anything. But if you examine your life, you will find there are lots of ways that you can simplify without feeling deprived. Realize the folly of desiring more and more luxuries bought on installment plans. Save up for what you need and pay for those needs outright—no installment plans with high interest to worry about. Of course, there is value in giving business to others who must sell their goods to make a living. But don't be enslaved by temptation to live beyond your means; for when you come to a tight corner, everything will be gone.

Save something out of each paycheck. To live without capital is a weakness courting disaster. Better to have a smaller car and home and some savings in the bank for emergencies, which are bound to come. It is a great mistake to spend all you receive just to get something new or luxurious. I think both husbands and wives independently should have a little nest egg in the bank, as well as a joint savings, on which they can rely when an unexpected need arises.

Saving is an art, and it requires sacrifice. But if you buy frugally, and live simply, you will be able to save something every week or month. I see so many workers who spend on unnecessary things, and consequently they are always in debt. I remember a couple who had a beautiful home in Florida. Whenever they saw something they liked they immediately bought it on the installment plan. But the time came when that home was only a terror in their minds. I said, "These are not your things. You don't own them. You have just borrowed them on installments. Why are you afraid to lose them? Why not live more simply without this constant worry that is destroying all your peace and enjoyment?" Because of their indebtedness, they did finally lose everything. They had to go back to the simple life and start all over again.

It is possible to enjoy vicariously so many of

the good and beautiful things in life without the terrible nervous depression of worry about how to pay for owning them. Lots of desires can be satisfied that way.

ANALYZE YOUR DESIRES
BEFORE ACTING ON THEM

A worthwhile desire is like a divine steed which, instead of leading you to the valley of darkness, will lead you toward the kingdom of God. Analyze each desire as to whether it will contribute to your spiritual welfare and betterment. Anything that leads you away from material enslavement to the kingdom of true happiness is the right kind of desire. Every motivation is good that brings forth a flower of God's manifest qualities and understanding. If anyone hurts you and you forgive him, you are leading yourself to the kingdom of God. If anyone is quarrelsome and you give understanding, you are taking yourself to the kingdom of God. If someone is suffering and you reach out with aid and compassion, you are moving into the presence of God.

True success is dependent on attainment of a proper desire—not when you are bent on acquisition at the cost of others' welfare. Riches achieved through reprehensible means may appear outwardly to be success; but inwardly your soul will not be at rest. Your conscience is like a shoe: When it doesn't fit, it may look nice outwardly; but no matter how carefully you walk, you know exactly where that shoe pinches. One who is good before his conscience is good before God as well. Do not stand convicted before your conscience. If your conscience is clear you can stand against the opinion of the world; no matter how dense the darkness around you, you shall pierce the gloom. Materially ambitious people pursue their passion for success and do not care if it comes by wrong means. Regardless of what they may achieve, they are never really successful, for they are never happy. If you want to succeed, do it in an honorable way.

True success achieves those things and fulfills those desires that are wholesome—beneficial to one's physical, mental, and spiritual welfare. As soon as you are confronted with some inner urge, ask whether that desire is wholesome or not. Know the difference between motivations that are good for you and those that are not. Use reason and discrimination when going after success in fulfilling your desires.

THE SUCCESSFUL PERSON IS CHARACTERIZED BY SELF-CONTROL

Harmless pleasures are all right; but those that hurt your mind and body are bad. Anything that enslaves you is not good. The power for our well-being and lasting happiness lies in self-control, in being able to do what we ought to do when we ought to do it, and in totally avoiding what we should not do. The successful person is characterized by self-control; he is unbound by whims and habits. To have complete mastery is to eat when and what you should eat; and when you shouldn't eat, you don't eat. When you want to mix with people, you mix wholeheartedly; and when you need time to be alone, you don't mix. If you use your time wisely in worthwhile activities, you and your life, as an extension of yourself, will be worthwhile. Worldly people want to sponge your time; they want to pull you to their level. Why settle for uselessness? Use your time in introspection for self-development, and in creative thinking and deep contemplation, and you will have great power over yourself.

If people persist in bothering you during your quiet times, or if you need respite from inharmonies at home, go to some peaceful place and stay alone for a while, listening to the soft sounds of nature and of God within. All the happiness you seek lies within you, in the image of God within you. Why settle for spurious imitations of happiness in drink, movies, and sensual gratifications? That is the way of the world. True happiness needs no supports. As a poet wisely philosophized: "Having nothing, yet having all."

REMAIN UNCONQUERED IN SPIRIT THROUGH ALL CHALLENGES AND TRIALS

You can learn to be happy at will and to hold on to that happiness within, no matter what happens. Some people are absolutely crushed by their tests; others smile on in spite of their difficulties. Those who are unconquered in spirit are the real successes in life. If you can so train or condition your mind that you are content regardless of what you have or do not have, and if you can stand the challenge of all your trials and remain calm — that is true happiness. Suppose you are suffering from a terrible disease; when you are asleep you are happily rid of it. Resolve to have that mental aboveness at all times; make up your mind to be happy at all costs. Jesus had such success in controlling his mind that he could willingly endure crucifixion and even resurrect his body after death. That was a demonstration of supreme success. His unconditional joy in God is the kind of success everyone is ultimately to achieve. It lies in owning yourself; when you, the soul, are able to be the boss of your life.

Say to your mind, "I am the boss; I am happy now, not tomorrow—when all the 'if' conditions are fulfilled." If you can command yourself to be happy at will, God will be with you, for He is the Fountainhead of all rivulets of joy. You don't know the power of the mind. If you are happy, it creates a positive vibratory attitude that can attract health and money and friends — everything you seek. Contrarily, when you are not happy, when you have a negative attitude, your will is paralyzed. Success in anything is dependent on being able to attract what you need by a strong, positive, happy will.

Analyze whether you have made a success of yourself. If you are habitually depressed, it is because you haven't made a success of your life. Things you have been wishing for years since childhood remain unfulfilled, and your morose mind has adopted a what's-the-use attitude. Revive your worthwhile goals with an energized will.

SUCCESS MEANS CREATIVE POWER TO ATTAIN WHAT YOU NEED

Success is not to be measured by how much material wealth is possessed, but whether you are able to create at will what you need. Think of that power; it comes from the superconscious mind, the infinite capacity of the soul. If you use that power to infuse your creative ability, you can overcome any difficulty that obstructs your path.

Suppose you need a car and you have the power to get it (by right means) — that is success. Suppose you need a house and you have the power to acquire it — you are successful. Suppose you want to have the right companion to share your life, and you pray to God to guide you and you meet that person — that is success. But how to go about achieving the power that makes for that kind of success at will? How to control the conditions that promote success instead of being controlled by your self-created cause-effect destiny? Very few in the world put forth enough determination and will to control their destiny.

Consider your immediate needs and always pray to God that you might have the creative power and will to meet them. Remember that man has not invented anything; he only discovers what God had already created in His ideations and made manifest in the causal world of thought from which all things in heaven and earth come into being. Therefore, the secret of success is to get more and more in tune with God.

THREE CREATIVE POWERS: THE CONSCIOUS, SUBCONSCIOUS, AND SUPERCONSCIOUS MINDS

You have three tremendous powers given to you by your Creator—your conscious mind, subconscious mind, and superconscious mind. You mostly use your conscious mind with its sensory input and its ability to reason. You are not that much acquainted with the other two minds, so their potential remains largely undeveloped.

Environment influences conscious effort. In a community someone creates a successful business and suddenly others see the area as holding a fertile opportunity to start similar rival businesses. As a result, some are bound to fail. One needs to employ all the power of discriminative reason at his command in considering the potential effects of environment in his field of endeavor. Ill-conceived hasty determinations are a sure formula for failure, and an insult to the willing-to-help abilities of the conscious mind.

There is always opportunity for success. Condition your conscious mind power to watch for opportunities—to recognize the little openings that take you where you want to go, and to seize those opportunities that are consistent with your goals.

By every honest effort, use your conscious mind to succeed. There is so much capacity in that mind—reason, discrimination, creative thought, will power, concentration. Search out opportunities by being more aware, and then apply yourself with concentration to your tasks. First, find out your abilities and then apply yourself. Whatever you are interested in, go after that; the seeds of success are best nurtured by an enthusiastic interest.

Do not get lost in wrong influences. The conscious mind is easily discouraged by the limitations imposed on it by environment and the suggestions of people. In the beginning I was considered useless by my family because I did not seek the offerings of the world. But I resisted their disparaging thoughts. As soon as you accept the limitations of external conditions and naysayers, your creativity and will to succeed become paralyzed. That is the analysis applicable to everyone who has failed in life.

USING THE INSTRUMENT OF THE SUBCONSCIOUS MIND

Next, in controlling destiny, is to employ the instrumentality of your subconscious mind; the mental faculty behind the conscious mind. That mind is the memory and habit mind. It stores all of your experiences and solidifies your thoughts and actions into habit patterns. Anything that you do with conscious attention, your subconscious mind saves in a blueprint in your brain. If you think you are a failure, a blueprint of failure is set in your subconscious mind. That preset conclusion is disastrous to the processes of success, a major reason for which people fail. No matter what your conditions in life, or the outcome of your efforts, you have no right to think failure, to hypnotize your mind with that belief.

Whatever you want to accomplish, affirm and believe in its attainment, in spite of contrary evidence. Create the pattern of success in your subconscious mind and make it work for you. Sit quietly and think deeply about your goal; concentrate on how to attain it. When you are still, when your restless and "can't do it" thoughts quiet down, the new convictions in your subconscious mind can help you. As you go deep into thought and begin to think a problem through, you go beyond the limits of the conscious mind and can feed into the conscious processes of reason valuable information from the memories and from the imaginative creativity of the subconscious mind.

THE ALL-KNOWING POWER OF THE SUPERCONSCIOUS MIND

Behind the subconscious mind is the superconscious mind. The power of God within you, the power of limitless control, lies in the superconscious mind. That mind cannot be suggested with failure, but it can be eclipsed by the suggestion of failure. The superconscious mind is the all-knowing intuitive consciousness of the soul. That mind can be tapped in deep concentration and in soul-contact in meditation.

Remind yourself always, no matter what

comes, "I have the power to succeed. And though the conscious mind is conditioned to my environment, the Lord has given me unlimited power in the superconscious mind and the subconscious mind. As I begin to control them, I shall be able to control my destiny." There is no jinx in your destiny except in lack of application of the powers of your conscious mind, and in the bad habits ingrained in your subconscious mind. You must never be discouraged; to be discouraged is to admit failure, to trademark yourself with failure. If your conscious mind says, "I can't do it," the subconscious mind records that failure thought; and the more you think negatively, the deeper you drive that failure idea into the library of your subconscious mind. Then you are done for—unless you again make the conscious effort to do away with the persistent conviction of failure by taking positive steps to think and act with a confident will.

When you think, "I can succeed," think it so deeply that you drive out any notion of failure. If nine times you try to succeed, but you fail, still you can try the tenth time! Do not give up; never admit failure.

PRACTICAL APPLICATION OF INTUITION

Begin every venture by asking for God's help: "Lord, I shall try my utmost, but guide me to do the right thing and to avoid mistakes." Then you must use your intelligence and reason to determine how to accomplish what you want to achieve. At every step, pray to God for guidance; feel His assurance in the intuition of inner calmness. That is what I do. After I use the intelligence of my conscious mind, I use my intuitive power as well as the other powers of my subconscious and superconscious minds; and I see that the creative divine light comes to guide me, without fail.

There is always uncertainty in depending only on the material ways of success. But the intuitive way of success is different. Intuitive perception can never be wrong. It comes by an inner sensitivity, a feeling by which you know in advance whether or not you are going to succeed by following your determined course.

The testimony of the senses and the rational mind may tell you one thing while the testimony of the intuition tells you otherwise. You should follow the testimony of the senses first—learn all you can about your goal and the practical steps needed to achieve it. Whether you are investing your money, starting a business, changing your occupation, after you have investigated, compared, and applied your intelligence to the limit, don't rush headlong into it. When your reason and investigation points to one thing, then meditate and pray to God. In inner silence, ask the

Lord if it is all right to go ahead. If you pray deeply and earnestly and find that something is turning you from it, don't do it. But if you have an irresistible positive impulse, and you pray and pray and go on praying and this impulse still persists, then go ahead. Your prayer for guidance must be sincere, so that whatever impulse you feel will be from God and not mere reinforcement of your own flawed desire.

That is the way I developed the practical application of my intuition. Before starting any endeavor, I sit in meditative silence in my room and go on expanding that power in my mind. Then I throw the concentrated light of my mind on what I want to accomplish. I know my thoughts have worked; what I perceive in that state must come to pass.

After all, we are the most powerful of receiving and broadcasting stations. The little barrier of flesh means nothing. Our thoughts are powerful creative forces floating in the ether ready to accomplish their purpose when they are concentrated and consciously directed. But most persons do not know how to make their thoughts work for them. Their minds are full of static. Concentration and meditation tunes those thoughts and focuses them on manifesting success.

ENLARGE YOUR SUCCESS BY HELPING OTHERS TO HELP THEMSELVES

A selfish agenda limits success. You should express the universal consciousness of your soul. You don't have to work only through the hands and brain of your own body. You can make your influence so widely felt that your goodness works through thousands of hands and brains. You think of your little body, how to feed, clothe, and give it comfort. I think of how to better the lives of thousands of souls, of being successful in giving people their own power of strength and wisdom. The satisfaction this gives is beyond words.

The success I have found in helping people to help themselves is a success that no one can destroy. It has been fun to do things for God. I have no ambition for myself, but I have much ambition for God, and for sharing Him with all. Unless you sacrifice some of your desires for the welfare of others, you can never be a real success. If you include the welfare of others in your efforts to succeed, you have a greater chance to be successful than if you think only of yourself. And above all else think of God and ask Him to guide you. I would have had a lot more trouble with the building of this society if I had not received inner divine direction, because each one who came wanted me to do it his way. This organization will succeed because I have followed God's way. Satan always tries to obstruct good works, but God shows the way to overcome all evils.

THE ULTIMATE SUCCESS: TO BE WITH GOD ALL THE TIME

Our purpose in life is to know the meaning of this universe. It is only a dream of God, just like a motion picture, which reveals great drama or comedy and then is over and forgotten. So is life. It seems so real and so permanent, but it will be over with shortly. All your problems and struggles will be forgotten when you leave this world for the better world of the afterlife. So do not take this life too seriously; look behind this drama to the Master of this universe, the Author of this dream play.

Many people say, "I will never be able to realize God." That is the hardest thought to remove. But as you pray and pray and never mind how many times God does not answer, if still you pray, still you love Him, then only will you succeed. Even eons of seeking God are nothing compared to eternity with Him. When you continuously pour out your heart in demanding God-realization, you will surely find His answer.

Do not waste your time. The way to true success is to be with God all the time. Seek Him first. Do not remain stagnant; laziness is not happiness. At night be with Him. And awaken in the morning ready to battle with the world, with Him by your side. With faith in your power to succeed say, "Come along, world. I am ready!" You will control your destiny; one by one your shackles will fall away. You will know that you are no longer a prodigal wanderer on earth, but that you have reclaimed your heritage as a son of God.

The only reason I am here with you is to declare what God has given to me. Finding the Supreme Power, I found the thirst of all my desires quenched forever. Don't delay; follow these teachings, that you may feel the wonderful things I have felt on this path. It has not only given me complete harmony in body and mind, but also contentment and happiness indescribable, and His constant guidance. You shall feel His presence in the caressing breeze; you shall see His bursting ever-new joy in the ocean; He will warm you in the sunshine. He will watch you through the overarching sky; and the heavenly bodies of stars and moon and sun will be windows to His presence. From His everywhereness you will see His benign eyes peering at you with love.

Every morning when you begin your day, think not only of serving your own welfare, but of how many others you can help.... If you are all interested in truth as much as I am, how great shall be our power to banish ignorance from the world. Everything that you do to help others in the way of this spiritual path will be remembered by the Father.

FEEL THE POWER OF SPIRIT MOVING THROUGH YOU

Now, close your eyes and concentrate within. Feel great peace within you. Feel peace all around you. Feel the power of Spirit moving through the calm portals of your mind; feel the peaceful glow of the Father within. He is hiding in every thought, in every cell, in everything within you. Feel Him.

Let us pray: "Heavenly Father, I am no longer surrounded by barriers of 'I can't.' I have within me Thy great explosive power of 'I can!' Lord, bless me that I develop that power, so that I may destroy all my barriers and expand my territory beyond the limitations of my existence until I conquer the forces of this earth and of Thy cosmos by being one with Thee."

PART II

How to Find a Way to Victory

This earth, which once seemed such a big place, I behold now as a tiny ball of atoms, spinning in space, warmed by sunshine, with nebulous gases playing around it—a little ball of clay on which various life forms grow. The Word of God, the Voice of Spirit — the manifestation of

Extracts from a talk given on February 16, 1939. The complete talk appears in *The Divine Romance* (Paramahansa Yogananda's *Collected Talks and Essays*, Volume II), published by Self-Realization Fellowship.

the Infinite—is in everything.* The disastrous upheavals that take place on this finite sphere are caused by human selfishness; by man's inharmony with man, and with the hidden Spirit in man and in all creation. Because mankind has not learned the lesson of these catastrophes, the earth continues to suffer devastating storms, earthquakes, floods, diseases, and worse than these, the clouds of war.

There is a way to conquer this world—to conquer nature and to conquer life, with its poverty, disease, wars, and other troubles. We must learn this way to victory....The world is

---

* Cosmic Intelligent Vibration, which structures and enlivens all creation; also referred to as *Aum* or Amen. *Aum* of the Vedas became the sacred word *Hum* of the Tibetans; *Amin* of the Moslems; and *Amen* of the Egyptians, Greeks, Romans, Jews, and Christians. "In the beginning was the Word, and the Word was with God, and the Word was God.... All things were made by him [the Word or *Aum*]; and without him was not any thing made that was made" (John 1:1,3).

marching on in a wild drama of existence. Trying to stop the raging storms, we seem no more than little ants swimming in the ocean. But do not minimize your power. The real victory consists in conquering yourself, as did Jesus Christ. His self-victory gave him power over all nature.

Science approaches the mastery of nature and of life in another way. Yet the initial promise of scientific discoveries often fails to yield anything permanent. The beneficial effects are felt only for a little while; then something worse comes along to threaten man's happiness and well-being. Total victory will not come by applying the methods of science alone, because these methods deal with externals, with effects rather than their subtle causes. The world will go on in spite of disasters, and science will again and again make new conquests. But only spiritual science can teach us the way to complete victory.

THE MIND MUST REMAIN UNDEFEATED

According to spiritual science, the attitude of the mind is everything. It is sensible to conquer extreme heat by the use of artificially cooled air, and extreme cold by artificially produced warmth; but while trying to conquer discomfort externally, train the mind to remain neutral to every condition. Mind is just like blotting paper, which readily takes on the color of any dye you apply to it. Most minds take on the color of their environment. But there is no excuse for the mind to be defeated by outer circumstances. If your mental attitude changes constantly under the pressure of tests, you are losing the battle of life. This is what happens when someone in good health and with a good mind goes out into the world to earn a living and immediately gives in to failure when he meets a few obstacles. It is when you *accept* failure that you *are* a failure. Not he who is handicapped by illness, nor he who is constantly trying in spite of repeated setbacks, but he who is physically and mentally lazy is the real failure. The person who refuses to think, or reason, or discriminate, or use his will or creative energy, is already dead.

Learn how to use the psychology of victory. Some people advise, "Don't talk about failure at all." But that alone won't help. First, analyze your failure and its causes, benefit from the experience, and then dismiss all thought of it. Though he fail many times, the man who keeps on striving, who is undefeated within, is a truly victorious person. No matter if the world considers him a failure; if he has not given up mentally, he is not defeated before the Lord. This truth I have learned from my contact with Spirit.

You are always comparing your lot with that of others. Someone is more alert and successful than you are; therefore you are miserable. This is a paradox of human nature. Don't bemoan your fate. The minute you enviously compare what you have with what someone else has, you defeat yourself. If you only knew the minds of others, you wouldn't want to be anyone but who you are!

We should envy no one. Let others envy us. What we are, no one else is. Be proud of what you have and what you are. No one else has a personality just like yours. No one else has a face like yours. No one else has a soul like yours. You are a unique creation of God. How proud you should be!

THE YOGA SCIENCE OF REMOVING WRONG THOUGHTS

To say there is no evil is unrealistic. We cannot escape evil by ignoring it. What is evil? Anything that obstructs God-realization. God is aware of all our wrong thoughts and doings and the troubles we are in. If He doesn't know that evil exists, He must be a very ignorant God! So, good and evil, the positive and the negative, both exist in this world. While trying to keep the consciousness positive, many people become unreasonably afraid of negative thoughts. It is useless to deny that negative thoughts exist, but neither should you fear them. Use your discrimination to analyze wrong thoughts; and then dump them.

Once the poison of a negative thought takes hold in the ego,* it is very hard to get rid of. A story is told of a man who was trying to drive an evil spirit out of a woman. He threw mustard seed at her, which was supposed to make the spirit depart. But the evil spirit just laughed: "I got into the mustard seed before you threw it, so it doesn't work against me." Similarly, when the poison of negative thoughts has thor-

---

* Human consciousness, identified with the body and hence with mortal limitations. The divine consciousness of the soul is identified with God and is impervious to negative influences.

oughly permeated your mind, the power of the mind doesn't work anymore. The "evil spirit" of negative thoughts gets into the "mustard seed" of your mental force. Thus, if you have been sick for a month, you tend to think you are going to be sick always. How can that one month of illness outweigh the fact of the many years of good health you have enjoyed? Such reasoning is unfair to your mind.

Deep metaphysicians probe into the consciousness of the soul, and with its divine power drive out all traces of evil from their lives. This is the yoga way of destroying all obstacles to the union of soul with God; it is not imaginary, but scientific. Yoga is the highest way to God. Through yoga you leave behind all negative thoughts and realize the ultimate states of consciousness. Yoga is the path of the spiritual scientist. It is pure science throughout, a complete science. Yoga teaches you to look yourself honestly in the eye and find out what you are, and then, with all the strength of your soul, to destroy the evil in you. You cannot just deny evil away. No matter how much persistence it takes, the spiritual scientist is never discouraged. He knows there is no trouble formidable enough to overpower the strength the Lord has given him.

ANALYZE YOURSELF HONESTLY SO YOU CAN IMPROVE

Learn to analyze yourself, looking at both the negative and the positive: how did you come to be what you are? what are your good and bad points, and how did you acquire them? Then set about to destroy the bad harvest. Remove the tares of evil traits from your soul and sow more seeds of spiritual qualities, to increase the crop of good harvest. As you recognize your weaknesses and scientifically remove them, you become stronger. Therefore you must not allow yourself to be discouraged by your frailties; to do so is to acknowledge yourself a failure. You must be able to help yourself by constructive self-analysis. Those who don't exercise their discriminative faculty are blind; the native wisdom of the soul has been eclipsed by ignorance. This is why people suffer.

God has given us the power to remove ignorance and uncover our innate wisdom, just as He has given us the power to open our eyelids and perceive light. Introspect every night, and keep a mental diary; and now and then during the daytime be still for a minute, and analyze what you are doing and thinking. Those who don't analyze themselves never change. Growing neither smaller nor bigger, they stagnate. This is a dangerous state of existence.

You become stagnant when you let circumstances override your better judgment. It is all too easy to waste time and forget about the kingdom of God. Thus you dwell too much on petty things, and have no time to think about Him. When you analyze yourself each night, be watchful that you are not becoming stagnant. You came into the world not to lose yourself, but to find your true Self. God sent you here as His soldier to win victory over your life. You are His child, and the greatest sin is to forget or to put off your highest duty: to win the victory over your little self and regain your true place in the kingdom of God.

THE CONQUEST OF SELF
IS THE GREATEST VICTORY

The greater your troubles, the greater the chance you have to show the Lord that you are a spiritual Napoleon or a spiritual Genghis Khan —a conqueror of your self. There are so many imperfections within us to be surmounted! He who becomes master of himself is a real conqueror. You must strive to do what I am doing — constantly winning within myself. And in this inner victory, I find the whole world at my command. The elements, which seem so mysterious, the scriptures, which seem so contradictory—all things are made clear in the great light of God. In that Light everything is understood and mastered. To gain this wisdom of God is the only purpose for which you were sent here; and if you seek anything else instead, you are going to punish yourself. Find your Self and find God. And whatever life demands of you, do it to the best of your ability. By discrimination, by right action, learn to conquer every obstacle and attain self-mastery.

So long as you question whether you will win or lose in your battles with life, you will go on losing. But when you are intoxicated with the happiness of God within you, you become more positive—and more humble. Don't go backward, and don't stand still. The majority are either stationary or engaged in a tug-of-war between their good and evil tendencies.

Which will win? Temptation is the voice of Satan whispering within your mind. Satan is always trying to bungle matters for you. To be stricken with weakness is not a sin, but the minute you give up the effort to overcome it, you are lost. So long as you are trying, so long as you pick yourself up when you fall, you will succeed. It is not the victory itself that brings pleasure, but the power and the satisfaction that come when you conquer a weakness.

Study the lives of the saints. That which is easy to do is not the way of the Lord. That which is difficult to do is His way! Saint Francis had more troubles than you could imagine, but he didn't give up. One by one, by the power of mind, he overcame those obstacles and became one with the Master of the Universe. Why shouldn't you have that kind of determination? I often think that the most sinful action in life is to admit failure, for in doing so, you deny the supreme power of your soul, God's image within you. Never give up.

Develop a liking for those pursuits that will help you to have greater mastery over yourself. Real victory is to carry out your good resolutions in spite of all difficulties. Let nothing break your determination. Most people reason, "Let it go today; I will try again tomorrow." Don't deceive yourself. That kind of thinking will not bring victory. If you make a resolution and never cease trying to carry it out, you will succeed. Saint Teresa of Avila said, "Saints are sinners who never gave up." Those who never surrender eventually attain victory.

BE SECURE IN YOUR INNATE GOODNESS

One day you will be gone from this world. Some will cry for you, and some may say a few words against you. But remember that all the bad thoughts you have had, as well as your good ones, will go with you. So your important duty is to watch yourself, correct yourself, do your best. Ignore what others may say or do against you, so long as you are sincerely striving to do right. I try never to antagonize anyone, and within my heart I know I have done my utmost to be kind to all. But I care not about man's opinion, whether praise or condemnation. God is with me, and I am with Him.

It isn't a boast, but I have experienced in my own consciousness the great joy of the sure feeling in my soul that no one can provoke me to revenge. I would rather slap myself than be mean to anyone. If you hold to your determination to be kind, no matter how people try to ruffle you, you are a conqueror. Think about it. When you are threatened, and you remain calm and unafraid, know that you are victorious over your little self. Your enemy cannot touch your spirit.

I could not think of being unkind, even to a mortal enemy. It would hurt me. I see so much unkindness in the world, and there is no excuse for me to add to it. When you love God, and when you see God in every soul, you cannot be mean. If someone behaves hurtfully toward you, think of the best ways to behave lovingly toward him. And if he still refuses to be considerate, remain withdrawn for a time. Keep your kindness locked up within, but let no demonstration of unkindness mar your behavior. One of the greatest victories over the little self is to be sure of your capacity to be always thoughtful and loving, to be secure in the knowledge that no one can make you act differently. Practice this. The entire Roman government could not have roused unkindness in Christ. Even for those who crucified him, he prayed: "Father, forgive them; for they know not what they do."*

When you are certain of your self-com-

* Luke 23:34.

mand, your victory is greater than a dicta-
tor's—a victory that stands immaculate before
the tribunal of your conscience. Your conscience is your judge. Let your thoughts be the
jury and you the defendant. Put yourself to
the test every day, and you will find that as
often as you take punishment at the hands of
your conscience, and as often as you strictly
sentence yourself to be positive—to be true to
your divine nature—you will be victorious.

ATTAINING THE VICTORY OF THE SOUL

Age is no excuse for not trying to change
oneself. Victory lies not in youth but in persistence. Cultivate the persistence that Jesus
had. Compare his mentality, when the time
came for him to give up his body, with that of
any seemingly successful free man walking
the streets of Jerusalem. To the very end, in
every test—even when Jesus was imprisoned
and crucified by his enemies—he was su-

premely victorious. He had power over all nature; and he played with death to conquer death. Those who fear it allow death to be victorious over them. But those who face themselves, and try every day to change for the better, will face death with courage and win the true victory. It is this victory of the soul that is most important.

For me there is no longer any veil between life and death, so death doesn't frighten me at all. The embodied soul is like a wave on the ocean. When someone dies, the soul-wave subsides and vanishes beneath the surface of the ocean of Spirit, whence it came. The truth about death is secreted from the consciousness of ordinary people, who make no effort to realize God. Such persons cannot conceive that within themselves is the kingdom of God, replete with His wonders. There, no pain, no poverty, no worries, no nightmares, can ever delude the soul. All I have to do is open my spiritual eye, and the earth is gone and another world appears. In that land I behold the infinite God. This state comes through a balance between activity and meditation. Tremendous activity is necessary; not with a desire to serve oneself, but with a desire to serve God. And equally necessary is daily effort to realize Him through deep meditation.

HARMONIZING WORLDLY DUTIES AND YOUR SEARCH FOR GOD

Your being a very busy person does not justify your forgetting God. Devotees on the spiritual path have even more tests than those who follow a material path, so don't use your worldly obligations as an excuse to ignore God.

You should not neglect God for work, and you should not neglect work for God. You must harmonize both activities. Meditate every day, and be thinking of God as you carry your heavy bag of worldly duties. Feel that you are doing everything to please Him. If you are busy for God, then no matter what tasks you are performing, your mind will be always on Him.

In the difficult struggle to maintain balance between meditation and activity, the greatest safety lies in the consciousness of the Lord. Everything that I do with the consciousness of God becomes meditation. Those who habitually drink can work while they remain under the influence of the alcohol. So, if you are habitually intoxicated with God, you can work without interrupting your inner divine communion. In the state of deep meditation, when your mind has withdrawn from everything and you are one with the consciousness of God, no stray thought will cross the threshold of your memory. You will stand with God behind the strong iron gate of your concentration and devotion, which neither gods nor goblins dare pass through. That is the most wondrous state of victory!

Get away from everyone now and then, just to be with God. See no one. Introspect, study, and meditate. Night is the best time for such seclusion. You may think you can't change your habits and practice this because so many duties occupy your time. But you have the whole night to yourself, so there is no excuse not to seek God. Don't be afraid you will lose your health if you lose a little sleep. Through deep meditation you will gain greater health.

After a certain hour at night, my mind is not with the world at all; I am mentally away from everything. Sleep is a very small consideration in my life. At night I try to feel sleepy like others; I tell myself I will sleep; but a great Light comes, and all thought of sleep vanishes. When I don't sleep, I never miss it. In eternal wakefulness I see there is no sleep. The joy of divine wisdom enthralls the consciousness.

I feel the drama of God that no one else can feel, save those to whom He reveals Himself. I am part of this world drama, and I am apart from it. I behold you all as actors in this cosmic play. The Lord is the director. Although you have been cast in a particular role, He has not made you an automaton. He wants you to perform intelligently and with concentration, and with the realization that you are playing your role for no one but Him. This is how you should think. God has chosen you for a specific work in this world, and whether you are a businessman or a housekeeper or a laborer, play your part to please Him alone. Then you will be victorious over the sufferings and limitations of this world. He who has God in his bosom has all the powers of the angels within him. His victory cannot be stayed.

When you are moving blindly through the valley of life, stumbling in darkness, you need the help of someone who has eyes. You need a guru. To follow one who is enlightened is the only way out of the great muddle that has been created in the world.... The real way to freedom lies in yoga, in scientific self-analysis, and in following one who has traversed the forest of theology and can lead you safely to God....

TO WIN GOD IS THE ULTIMATE VICTORY

So remember, don't think you cannot change and improve. Every night, analyze yourself; and meditate deeply, praying: "Lord, I have lived too long without You. I have played enough with my desires. Now what is to become of me? I must have You. Come to my aid. Break Your vow of silence. Guide me." Ten times He may remain silent; but in between, when you least expect it, He will come to you. He cannot remain away. So long as you harbor an unholy curiosity He will not come; but if you are really sincere, then no matter where you are, He will be with you. This is worth all the effort you may make.

Seclusion is the price of greatness. Avoid going too often into noisy places. Noise and restless activity keep the nerves excited with emotion. That isn't the way to God; it is the way to destruction, for that which destroys your peace draws you away from God. When you are calm and quiet, you are with the Lord. I try to remain by myself most of the time, but whether I am alone or in crowds, I find seclusion in my soul. Such a deep cave! All the sounds of the earth fade away, and the world becomes dead to me, as I stroll in my cave of peace. If you haven't found this inner kingdom, why are you wasting your time? Who will save you? None but yourself. So lose no more time.

Even if you are crippled, blind, deaf, dumb, and forsaken by the world, don't you give up! If you pray, "Lord, I cannot go to Thy temple because of my helpless eyes and limbs, but with all my mind I am thinking of Thee," then the Lord comes and says: "Child, the world gives you up, but I take you in My arms. In My eyes you are victorious." I live in the glory of that consciousness of His presence every day. I feel a wonderful detachment from everything else. Even when I try to feel a special wish for something, I find my mind detached. Spirit is my food; Spirit is my joy; Spirit is my feeling; Spirit is my temple and my audience; Spirit is my library, whence I draw inspiration; Spirit is my love and my Beloved. The spirit of God is the satisfier of all my desires, for in Him I find all wisdom, all the love of a beloved, all beauty, all everything. There is no other desire, no other ambition left for me, but God. Whatever I sought, I found in Him. So will you find.

EACH SPIRITUAL EFFORT YOU MAKE BRINGS AN EVERLASTING GIFT OF THE SOUL

Waste no more time, for if you have to change your bodily residence you will have to wait a long time for another opportunity to seek God earnestly, passing first through rebirth and the travails of childhood and the restlessness of youth. Why squander your time in useless desires? It is foolish to spend your life seeking things you must forsake at death. You will never find happiness that way. But every effort you make toward the contact of God in meditation will bring you an everlasting gift of the soul. Start now—those of you who are real lovers of God, seeking not your own glory, but the glory of Spirit.

Each one has to win his own victory. Make up your mind that you are going to be supremely victorious. You don't need an army or money or any other material help to gain the highest victory attainable; just a strong determination that you are going to win. All you have to do is sit still in meditation, and with the sword of discrimination cut off, one by one, the advance of restless thoughts. When they will all be dead, God's kingdom of calm wisdom will be yours.

Every one of you who has heard this sermon, and who makes a sincere effort to change, will find a greater communion with God, and in Him the true and lasting victory of the spirit.

ABOUT THE AUTHOR

PARAMAHANSA YOGANANDA (1893–1952) is widely regarded as one of the preeminent spiritual figures of our time. Born in northern India, he came to the United States in 1920, where for more than thirty years he taught India's ancient science of meditation and the art of balanced spiritual living. Through his acclaimed life story, *Autobiography of a Yogi,* and his numerous other books, Paramahansa Yogananda has introduced millions of readers to the perennial wisdom of the East. Under the guidance of one of his earliest and closest disciples, Sri Daya Mata, his spiritual and humanitarian work is carried on by Self-Realization Fellowship, the international society he founded in 1920 to disseminate his teachings worldwide.

Also published by Self-Realization Fellowship…

AUTOBIOGRAPHY OF A YOGI
by Paramahansa Yogananda

This acclaimed autobiography is at once a riveting account of an extraordinary life and a penetrating and unforgettable look at the ultimate mysteries of human existence. Hailed as a landmark work of spiritual literature when it first appeared in print, it remains one of the most widely read and respected books ever published on the wisdom of the East.

With engaging candor, eloquence, and wit, Paramahansa Yogananda narrates the inspiring chronicle of his life—the experiences of his remarkable childhood, encounters with many saints and sages during his youthful search throughout India for an illumined teacher, ten years of training in the hermitage of a revered yoga master, and the thirty years that he lived and taught in America. He records as well his meetings with Mahatma Gandhi, Rabindranath Tagore, Luther Burbank, the Catholic stigmatist Therese Neumann, and other celebrated spiritual personalities of East and West. Also included is extensive material that he added after the first edition came out in 1946, with a final chapter on the closing years of his life.

Considered a modern spiritual classic, *Autobiography of a Yogi* offers a profound introduction to the ancient science of yoga. It has been translated into many languages and is widely used in college and university courses. A perennial best-seller, the book has found its way into the hearts of millions of readers around the world.

"A rare account."
— THE NEW YORK TIMES

"A fascinating and clearly annotated study."
— NEWSWEEK

"There has been nothing before, written in English or in any other European language, like this presentation of Yoga."
— COLUMBIA UNIVERSITY PRESS

A World in Transition: Finding Spiritual Security in Times of Change *(Anthology—Paramahansa Yogananda and other monastics of Self-Realization Fellowship)*

Self-Realization Fellowship Lessons

The scientific techniques of meditation taught by Paramahansa Yogananda, including *Kriya Yoga*—as well as his guidance on all aspects of balanced spiritual living—are presented in the *Self-Realization Fellowship Lessons*. For further information, you are welcome to write for the free booklet, *Undreamed-of Possibilities*.

SELF-REALIZATION FELLOWSHIP
3880 San Rafael Avenue • Los Angeles, CA 90065-3298
TEL (323) 225-2471 • FAX (323) 225-5088

www.yogananda-srf.org